SEP 2 9 2015

ANKYLOSAURUS

by Susan H. Gray

Published by The Child's World®
1980 Lookout Drive • Mankato, MN 56003-1705
800-599-READ • www.childsworld.com

Acknowledgments
The Child's World®: Mary Berendes, Publishing Director
The Design Lab: Design
Heidi Schoof: Photo Research
Michael Miller and Sarah Miller: Editing

Content Adviser
Peter Makovicky, PhD, Curator • Field Museum, Chicago, Illinois

Original Cover Art
Todd S. Marshall

Photo Credits
© Albert Copley/Visuals Unlimited, Inc.: 8, 9; AMNH/Courtesy of the Vertebrate
Paleontology Archives, Division of Paleontology: 12; Bettmann/Corbis: 11, 13,
20; Charles V. Angelo/Science Source: 21; Francois Gohier/Science Source:
7, 10, 14, 15, 19, 22, 27; Joe Tucciarone/Science Source: 25; Jonathan Blair/
Corbis: 23; Kevin Schafer/Corbis: 6; Pete Oxford/Minden Pictures/Corbis: 18;
Sinclair Stammers/Science Source: 17; slobo/iStockphoto.com: design element
(paper); Stephen J. Krasemann/Science Source: 5

ISBN 9781631439766
LCCN 2014959646

Printed in the United States of America
Mankato, MN
July, 2015
PA02263

CONTENTS

CHAPTER ONE

Having to Eat and Run

The afternoon rain slowed to a sprinkle. Sunlight peeked through the clouds. An *Ankylosaurus* (an-kuh-low-SORE-uhss) stood in a patch of moss, slowly chewing away. He blinked as raindrops hit the heavy ridges above his eyes.

Ankylosaurus heard a loud splash behind him. He swung his heavy, clubbed tail, but he hit nothing. Another splash. He turned his head to look back. But with his thick armor, he could not turn far enough to see. Splash! *Ankylosaurus* started walking away on his stubby legs, then he sped up into a trot. His broad feet pounded the earth and splashed mud everywhere. For a big, heavy dinosaur, he was moving pretty fast!

Despite being a peaceful, plant-eating dinosaur, Ankylosaurus was a huge, armored tank of a fighter. It weighed about 4 to 6 tons and could hold its own against enemies thanks to its spike-covered body and battering-ram-like tail.

Because Ankylosaurus was built low to the ground, it had to eat lots of low-lying plants, such as ferns. This fossilized fern is one kind of plant that an Ankylosaurus would have munched on.

He reached a grove of trees and slowed to a stop. He was panting—his huge, leathery sides heaving. Here in the shade grew some delicious ferns. *Ankylosaurus* completely forgot why he had been running and buried his head in the plants. Meanwhile, back at the moss patch, birds kept splashing away in the puddles.

CHAPTER TWO

What Is an Ankylosaurus?

The *Ankylosaurus* is a dinosaur that lived from about 72 million to 65 million years ago. Its name is taken from Greek words that mean "stiff lizard" or "fused lizard." The name refers to the many bony plates that covered its back and tail. These were fused, or joined together, with its thick skin, making the animal stiff.

These rough, hard, bony plates covered almost every square inch of the Ankylosaurus. They helped fend off attacks from vicious **predators**, such as the Tyrannosaurus rex.

The only area of the Ankylosaurus that was not covered in tough, bony plates or pointy spines was its underbelly. Flipping it over was the only way to disarm the dinosaur.

The **reptile** had an excellent coat of armor. In addition to its heavy plates, it was covered with many short, thick spines. Rows of spines ran down the animal's back from the neck to the tail. *Ankylosaurus* might also have had another row of spines down each of its sides. Large spikes stuck out from its head. A hard, bony shelf above each eye protected the dinosaur's vision. *Ankylosaurus* even had bony eyelids.

For more protection, *Ankylosaurus* had a mighty "club." Its muscular tail ended in a thick clump of bone, which was covered with tough, leathery skin. The tail was flexible enough to swing this bony club from side to side. One good, forceful swing was enough to break the shin or foot of an attacker.

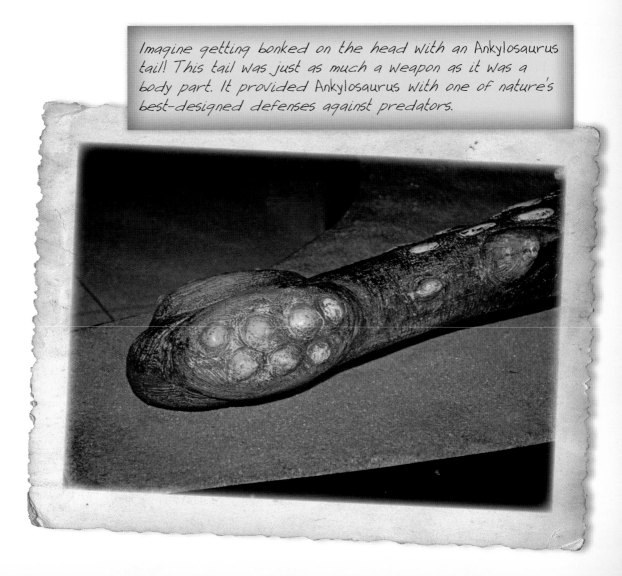

Imagine getting bonked on the head with an Ankylosaurus tail! This tail was just as much a weapon as it was a body part. It provided Ankylosaurus with one of nature's best-designed defenses against predators.

Ankylosaurus reached about 30 feet (9.1 meters) in length. It probably weighed between 4 and 6 tons. Its head was nearly 3 feet (0.9 m) long. Its skull bones were very thick, leaving little space for a brain.

The dinosaur walked on four mighty legs. The back legs were longer than the front legs, so the dinosaur's back sloped downward toward its head. Because of its body shape and thick armor, *Ankylosaurus* could not lift its head up very high. It

Ankylosaurus is not known for having been the smartest of the dinosaurs. In fact, its intelligence was low compared with other dinosaurs.

probably could not stand on its hind legs. *Ankylosaurus* was not built for attacking other dinosaurs. But it certainly was built to defend itself against them.

    Ankylosaurus bones were first discovered by a group of fossil hunters in Montana. A man named Barnum Brown led the group. Brown gave the dinosaur its name in 1908. So far, parts of three *Ankylosaurus* skeletons have been found in North America.

Notes of a Dinosaur Hunter

"Passed Wilbur Titus herding a band of sheep . . . he was just as dirty as ever . . . Pete and Lambert took wagon and Billy and went . . . to prospect *Ankylosaurus* quarry for more fragments . . . *Ankylosaurus*? skull + frags [fragments] 2 miles below Tolman ferry right bank 100 ft. above river . . . Loaded skull and got part way to ranch got stuck . . . . Took out *Ankylosaurus* frags . . . Rain + snow . . . Packed remaining boxes . . . Waited for roads to dry."

These are just a few of the writings in Barnum Brown's field notes. Good scientists always write plenty of notes when they are working. Scientists work in laboratories, in libraries, and out in nature. When they are working out in nature, they say they are "in the field." So their notes are called field notes.

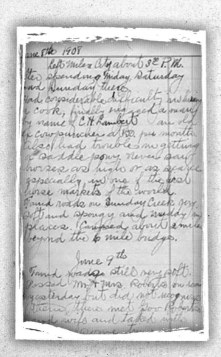

Brown (at left in the photograph) was one of the greatest dinosaur hunters ever. He began working for the American Museum of Natural History in New York when he was in his 20s. He got to travel all over the world searching for fossils. Brown always liked to dress nicely, even when he was working in the field. Everyone else would wear old clothes and get dirty, but not Brown. He wore a nice hat, coat, and tie in the field.

Brown led several crews on dinosaur hunts. They worked for years in Wyoming; Montana; and Alberta, Canada. With all this hard work, it is not surprising that he found so many fossils. He discovered not only *Ankylosaurus*, but also the first *Tyrannosaurus rex* (tie-ran-uh-SORE-uhss REX). Thanks to his field notes, we know what hard work it was to make these discoveries.

CHAPTER THREE

Dinosaur Diets

Several things about *Ankylosaurus* tell us that it was a plant-eater, or herbivore (UR-buh-vore). Its teeth were small and wide, not long and pointy. These teeth were good for grinding plant materials, not for biting meat. Its snout ended in a beak with a hard covering. Such a beak would have been good for

This fossil of an Araucaria cone is a key to the past. It helps scientists learn about what dinosaurs such as Ankylosaurus might have eaten. Fossils are nature's time capsules. They preserve the history of our planet for future generations to see.

tearing plants from the ground or leaves from bushes. The animal's heavy body, built close to the ground, would not have been fast enough to chase down **prey**.

Ankylosaurus was big and wide at the waist and hips. This also tells us that the animal ate plants. Plants contain a lot of material called cellulose (SELL-yoo-loce). Cellulose is difficult to digest.

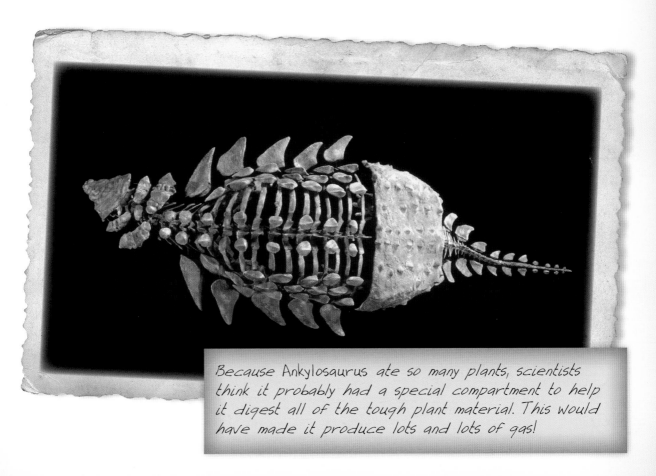

Because Ankylosaurus ate so many plants, scientists think it probably had a special compartment to help it digest all of the tough plant material. This would have made it produce lots and lots of gas!

Plant-eating animals have special **adaptations** (ad-ap-TAY-shuns) to help them digest cellulose. They may have an extra stomach or very long intestines. These take up lots of space in an animal's body. So the animal is big and wide. Because *Ankylosaurus* was so wide, scientists think it adapted to a diet of plants.

Ankylosaurus also had special adaptations to keep from being eaten. The bony plates and spines on its back were protection against the teeth and claws of predators. Smaller plates shielded its face and eyes. Only the animal's underside was unprotected. Its belly and throat had no spines at all. If *Ankylosaurus* was flipped over on its side or back, it would have been in trouble. But the animal was too heavy and low to the ground for most attackers to do this.

CHAPTER FOUR

Making Tracks

Paleontologists (pay-lee-un-TAWL-uh-jists) are people who study **ancient** plant and animal life. They often study fossils. These are remains of plants and animals that lived long, long ago. Dinosaur fossils include skeletons, eggs, and footprints. Until recently, most paleontologists thought *Ankylosaurus*

Paleontologists have found many fossilized dinosaur eggs at more than 200 sites in the United States, France, Spain, Argentina, India, Mongolia, and China.

People who want to know more about dinosaurs flock to Bolivia to get an up-close look at the dinosaur tracks. Imagine seeing the actual footprints of dinosaurs that once roamed that very land!

was a slow-moving dinosaur. They believed that something so big and heavy could only lumber along slowly. But in 1998, a paleontologist named Christian Meyer found footprints that told a different story. Meyer was leading a group of scientists on a field trip. They were in the South American country of Bolivia. There, they found a huge area covered with dinosaur trackways. Trackways are sets of dinosaur footprints. The area was more than 6 acres (2.4 hectares) in size. It quickly became famous for having the most dinosaur trackways in the world.

Meyer and his team counted more than 250 sets of footprints. They could tell that six kinds of dinosaurs had made the prints. They saw that some dinosaurs had been walking normally. Some had been limping. And some appeared to be trotting rather quickly.

The team decided that one of the footprints belonged to the group of dinosaurs called ankylosaurs (*Ankylosaurus* and its relatives). They figured that some were able to run at about 8 miles (12.8 kilometers) per hour.

Researchers who study dinosaur tracks say that tracks are the closest we can get to understanding dinosaurs as living, breathing animals. Tracks tell much about where and how dinosaurs walked, as well as which dinosaurs roamed alone and which moved in groups.

Studying Trackways

Paleontologists can tell a lot about a dinosaur just by looking at its tracks. If a big groove follows the footprints, they know the dinosaur dragged its tail as it walked. If one foot made a light print over and over, they know the dinosaur was limping.

If the dinosaur took extra long steps, scientists think it was probably running. Sometimes scientists study elephants and hippopotamuses to see how they run. They might measure the legs of these animals and compare them with dinosaur legs. They might check to see how

far apart the animals' footprints are. Scientists then use this knowledge to tell them about dinosaur footprints. It helps them figure out how fast dinosaurs could run.

The *Ankylosaur* trackways in Bolivia surprised the paleontologists. The tracks showed that this group of dinosaurs moved much faster than anyone had ever thought.

CHAPTER FIVE

Life in the Cretaceous Period

Ankylosaurus walked the earth during a time called the Cretaceous (kreh-TAY-shuss) period. The whole period lasted from 144 million years to 65 million years ago. But *Ankylosaurus* was around for only a few million years of that time.

Coelophysis (pronounced SEE-low-FIE-sis) was a small dinosaur with a tiny skull. It had a long, pointed head with lots of small teeth. Coelophysis lived in a period different from Ankylosaurus's period.

Dinosaurs first appeared on Earth about 230 million years ago. These were small creatures that ran on two legs. In time, more and more dinosaurs appeared. Some grew quite large. Some walked on four legs.

Snakes existed on Earth at the same time the dinosaurs did. Snakes first appeared during the late Cretaceous period (about 95 million years ago), toward the end of the time of the dinosaurs.

Ankylosaurus was one of the big, four-legged dinosaurs.

During the Cretaceous period, many reptiles roamed the earth. Dinosaurs, snakes, and lizards were common on the ground. Flying reptiles called pterosaurs (TEHR-uh-sorz) soared overhead. Swimming reptiles lived in the oceans.

Not all animals were reptiles, though. Small mammals, not much bigger than rats, darted about on the forest floor. Feathered birds flew from tree to tree. Sharks, rays, and other fish glided through the ocean waters.

CHAPTER SIX

So What Happened?

Something big happened at the end of the Cretaceous period, but no one knows what it was. Paleontologists tell us that 65 million years ago, dinosaurs became **extinct**. All over the world, they just died out. At about the same time, the pterosaurs, the reptiles of the sea, and many other animals disappeared. What could have caused this to happen?

Scientists have a few ideas. A lot of volcanoes were erupting at the end of the Cretaceous period. Perhaps this changed the air so much that dinosaurs could no longer breathe. Maybe the dinosaurs could not find enough food. Perhaps heat waves, diseases, or egg-eating mammals wiped out the dinosaurs. Over

Asteroids can be as small as pebbles or as large as 578 miles (930 km) in diameter. Sixteen of the 3,000 known asteroids are more than 150 miles (240 km) in diameter. Some asteroids even have their own orbiting moons.

the years, scientists have thought a lot about what killed all the dinosaurs.

There is one more idea that has gotten a lot of attention. Some scientists believe a giant **asteroid** crashed into Earth about 65 million years ago. They feel that such a crash could have caused many kinds of animals to die out. But how?

In the 1970s and 1980s, scientists began to notice something unusual in rocks from around the world. The rocks from about 65 million years ago had a lot of a material called iridium (ih-RID-eeum) in them. Iridium is very rare on Earth. But asteroids hurtling through space have plenty of it. If an asteroid slammed into Earth, it would release iridium over a huge area.

This is what many scientists believe happened 65 million years ago. A giant asteroid traveling at thousands of miles per hour crashed into Earth. The iridium and dust from the crash spread everywhere. Skies darkened, and many animals died.

This does not explain everything, though. It does not explain how plants survived. It does not explain why some animals lived on. The birds we know today, for example, are relatives of the dinosaurs. The birds survived, yet dinosaurs such as *Ankylosaurus* did not.

Why did the dinosaurs die out and birds like this condor stay alive? Paleontologists may never know, but mysteries like this make studying dinosaurs fun.

The mystery of the great extinction might never be answered. All we know is that something big happened 65 million years ago. And because of it, not a single dinosaur was left on Earth.

GLOSSARY

adaptations (ad-ap-TAYshuhnz) Adaptations are adjustments to something in the environment. Plant-eating animals have special adaptations to help them digest cellulose.

ancient (AYN-shunt) Something that is ancient is very old—from millions of years ago. Paleontology is the study of ancient plant and animal life.

asteroid (ASS-tuh-roid) An asteroid is a rocky body that is smaller than a planet and orbits the sun. A giant asteroid may have crashed into Earth millions of years ago and caused the dinosaurs to die out.

extinct (ek-STINGKT) Something that is extinct no longer exists. The dinosaurs became extinct about 65 million years ago.

predators (PRED-uh-turz) Predators are animals that hunt and eat other animals. The bony plates and spines of *Ankylosaurus* helped protect them from predators.

prey (PRAY) Prey are animals that are hunted and eaten by other animals. The bulky body of *Ankylosaurus* would have made it difficult for the dinosaur to chase after prey.

reptile (REP-tile) A reptile is an air-breathing animal with a backbone and is usually covered with scales or plates. *Ankylosaurus* was an example of a reptile.

TRIASSIC PERIOD

Date: 248 million to 208 million years ago
Fossils: *Coelophysis, Cynodont, Desmatosuchus, Eoraptor, Gerrothorax, Peteinoaurus, Placerias, Plateosaurus, Postosuchus, Procompsognathus, Riojasaurus, Saltopus, Teratosaurus, Thecodontosaurus*
Distinguishing Features: For the most part, the climate in the Triassic period was hot and dry. The first true mammals appeared during this period, as well as turtles, frogs, salamanders, and lizards. Corals could also be found in oceans at this time, although large reefs such as the ones we have today did not yet exist. Evergreen trees made up much of the plant life.

JURASSIC PERIOD

Date: 208 million to 144 million years ago
Fossils: *Allosaurus, Apatosaurus, Brachiosaurus, Compsognathus, Dilophosaurus, Diplodocus, Hybodus, Kentrosaurus, Megalosaurus, Saurolophus, Segisaurus, Seismosaurus, Stegosaurus, Supersaurus, Ultrasaurus, Vulcanodon*
Distinguishing Features: The climate of the Jurassic period was warm and moist. The first birds appeared during this period. Plant life was also greener and more widespread. Sharks began swimming in Earth's oceans. Although dinosaurs did not even exist at the beginning of the Triassic period, they ruled Earth by Jurassic times. A minor mass extinction occurred toward the end of the Jurassic period.

THE GEOLOGIC TIME SCALE

CRETACEOUS PERIOD

Date: 144 million to 65 million years ago
Fossils: *Alamosaurus, Albertosaurus, Ankylosaurus, Argentinosaurus, Bagaceratops, Baryonyx, Carnotaurus, Centrosaurus, Corythosaurus, Didelphodon, Edmontonia, Edmontosaurus, Gallimimus, Gigantosaurus, Hadrosaurus, Hypsilophodon, Iguanodon, Kronosaurus, Lambeosaurus, Maiasaura, Megaraptor, Nodosaurus, Oviraptor, Parasaurolophus, Protoceratops, Psittacosaurus, Saltasaurus, Sarcosuchus, Saurolophus, Sauropelta, Saurornithoides, Segnosaurus, Spinosaurus, Stygimoloch, Styracosaurus, Tarbosaurus, Thescelosaurus, Torosaurus, Trachodon, Triceratops, Troodon, Tyrannosaurus rex, Utahraptor, Velociraptor*
Distinguishing Features: The climate of the Cretaceous period was fairly mild. Flowering plants first appeared in this period, and many modern plants developed. With flowering plants came a greater diversity of insect life. Birds further developed into two types: flying and flightless. A wider variety of mammals also existed. At the end of this period came a great mass extinction that wiped out the dinosaurs, along with several other groups of animals.

DID YOU KNOW?

- *Ankylosaurus* trackways have been found in several places in the world. Except for the trackways in Bolivia, they all show that *Ankylosaurus* was a slow mover.

- *Ankylosaurus* had a very small brain for its body. Many scientists take this to mean that the dinosaur was not very smart.

- The full name of the dinosaur found by Barnum Brown is *Ankylosaurus magniventris* (MAG-nih-VEN-triss). This name means "stiff lizard with a big belly!"

HOW TO LEARN MORE

At the Library

Bailey, Gerry. *Ankylosaurus*. New York, NY: Crabtree, 2011.

West, David. *Ankylosaurus and Other Armored and Plated Herbivores*. New York, NY: Gareth Stevens, 2011.

On the Web

Visit our Web site for links about *Ankylosaurus*: **childsworld.com/links**

Note to Parents, Teachers, and Librarians: We routinely verify our Web links to make sure they are safe and active sites. So encourage your readers to check them out!

Places to Visit or Contact

American Museum of Natural History: *To view numerous dinosaur fossils, as well as the fossils of several ancient mammals*
Address: Central Park West at 79th Street, New York, NY 10024
Phone: (212) 769-5100

Carnegie Museum of Natural History: *To view a variety of dinosaur skeletons, as well as fossils related to other reptiles, amphibians, and fish that are now extinct*
Address: 4400 Forbes Avenue, Pittsburgh, PA 15213
Phone: (412) 622-3131

Dinosaur National Monument: *To view a huge deposit of dinosaur bones in a natural setting*
Address: 4545 East Highway 40, Dinosaur, CO 81610
Phone: (970) 374-3000
 –OR–
Dinosaur National Monument (Quarry):
Address: 11625 East 1500 South, Jensen, UT 84035
Phone: (435) 781-7700

Museum of the Rockies: *To see real dinosaur fossils, as well as robotic replicas*
Address: Montana State University, 600 West Kagy Boulevard, Bozeman, MT 59717
Phone: (406) 994-2251 or (406) 994-DINO

National Museum of Natural History (Smithsonian Institution): *To see several dinosaur exhibits and take special behind-the-scenes tours*
Address: 10th Street and Constitution Avenue, N.W., Washington, DC 20560
Phone: (202) 357-2700

INDEX

ABOUT THE AUTHOR

Susan H. Gray has bachelor's and master's degrees in zoology and has taught college-level courses in biology. She first fell in love with fossil hunting while studying paleontology in college. In her 25 years as an author, she has written many articles for scientists and researchers, and many science books for children. Susan enjoys gardening, traveling, and playing the piano. She and her husband, Michael, live in Cabot, Arkansas.